One Wing's Gift

Rescuing Alaska's Wild Birds

Joan Harris

ALASKA NORTHWEST BOOKS™

ANCHORAGE ❖ PORTLAND

*For Nana,
who taught me
to love all wild
creatures, and
for my mother,
Martha, who
always believed
I could draw.*

*A portion of the
proceeds from
this book will be
donated to the
Bird Treatment
and Learning
Center in
Anchorage,
Alaska.*

ACKNOWLEDGMENTS—Many people have helped to shape this book. Dr. James Scott provided unfailing encouragement. Special thanks also go to Bird TLC's caretakers; photographers Danny Simmons, Richard Bass, William Amos, Barbara Doak, and Dr. James Scott; and, for editorial guidance, LuAnne Dowling and Linda Gunnarson. Dr. Jane Evanson provided inspiration and encouragement. Thank you to the staff of the Education Center at Fort Richardson, who are more like kin than coworkers; and to my family, both near and far, especially my husband and best friend, Tom.

Text and illustrations © 2002 by Joan Harris
Author photo © 2002 by David Jensen
Copyright to photographs used as reference material by the artist belongs to the photographers listed in the Artist's Notes, beginning on page 63.
Published by Alaska Northwest Books™
An imprint of Graphic Arts Center Publishing Company
P.O. Box 10306, Portland, Oregon 97296-0306, 503-226-2402
www.gacpc.com

The quotation on page 5 is reprinted by permission of the publishers and the Trustees of Amherst College from *The Poems of Emily Dickinson*, Thomas H. Johnson, ed., Cambridge, Mass.: The Belknap Press of Harvard University Press, © 1951, 1955, 1979 by the President and Fellows of Harvard College.

Library of Congress Cataloging-in-Publication Data

Harris, Joan, 1946-
    One wing's gift : rescuing Alaska's wild birds / by Joan Harris.
        p. cm.
    ISBN 0-88240-560-8
        I. Birds, Protection of—Alaska. 2. Wildlife rescue—Alaska. 3. Bird Treatment and
Learning Center. 4. Birds—Alaska. I. Title.

    QL676.56.A4 H37 2002
    333.95'816'09798—dc21

                                                    2001046099

President / Publisher: Charles M. Hopkins
Associate Publisher: Douglas A. Pfeiffer
Editorial Staff: Timothy W. Frew, Ellen Harkins Wheat, Tricia Brown, Jean Andrews, Kathy Matthews, Jean Bond-Slaughter
Production Staff: Richard L. Owsiany, Susan Dupere
Cover Design: Elizabeth Watson
Interior Design: Paulette Livers, Livers Lambert Design
Copy Editor: Linda Gunnarson

Printed on acid- and elemental chlorine-free recycled paper in Singapore.

Contents

INTRODUCTION

The Rescuers

All the birds depicted in this book have passed through the doors of the
Bird Treatment and Learning Center (TLC) in Anchorage, Alaska, and have been
tended by its volunteers. The organization was founded in 1988 by longtime Alaska
veterinarian James Scott. It grew out of Dr. Scott's years-long love of and experience
with wild birds and his desire to help them. Long before Bird TLC was established,
the common knowledge around Anchorage was that Dr. Scott would willingly care
for such needy creatures. Many a person appeared on his steps carrying a feathered
bundle, and not one was turned away.

Originally working out of Dr. Scott's own Arctic Animal Hospital, Bird TLC
soon found itself providing emergency care for bald eagles injured in the 1989 *Exxon
Valdez* oil spill. The organization's flight pens at Fort Richardson were erected shortly
afterward, providing a facility where recovering bald eagles could practice their aerial
skills before being released back to the wild. In time, the scope of Bird TLC's rescue
work expanded to include rehabilitation of all feathered species, and more space was
badly needed. Relocating to a large vacant warehouse solved the problem. Taking
shape after countless volunteer hours, the interior of the cavernous building was
transformed to meet the specific requirements of a bird rescue center.

Today, large wooden cages with wire doors house birds of prey, called raptors.
These include hawks, eagles, falcons, and owls. Smaller enclosures accommodate even
tiny birds, and special water tanks help ducks and geese feel more at home. Outdoor
cages provide comfortable areas for snowy owls and other birds whose ideal room

temperature is very different from our own. A space for food preparation contains refrigerators and freezers well stocked with required staples of mice, quail, and salmon, and the all-important treatment areas are orderly and scrubbed.

Throughout this evolution, Dr. Jim Scott's vision has been a common thread. Donating his skills as veterinarian, he continues to help provide medical treatment to stabilize and rehabilitate diseased and injured birds. A private, nonprofit organization, Bird TLC uses volunteers to staff the clinic. The number of resident birds varies seasonally, but one constant is the abundance of willing human hands.

Always, the goal is release; but when a severe injury, such as to a bird's head or wing, prevents that, a permanent placement is found. Considering foremost the needs of each individual bird, this might be in a university breeding facility or even a volunteer's home. The trained volunteers in Bird TLC's education program take a variety of nonreleasable "teaching birds" to classrooms, local organizations, and community events. This increases public awareness of wild birds and encourages preservation of their habitat. Fitted with "jesses," teaching birds can be safely restrained on their caretaker's glove, as the leash-like jesses slip through a grommet on the bird's leather leg bands, and wind securely through the handler's fingers. These creatures serve as ambassadors of their kind, and their caretakers spend a great deal of time building the trust needed to help the birds feel comfortable on such educational forays.

Some months after the 1989 oil spill, I had a chance to visit the Bird TLC flight pens constructed for the recuperating eagles at Fort Richardson. I had no idea how deeply the visit would affect me or how it would eventually change the direction of my art. I have always loved wild birds, so I was thrilled with an opportunity to see firsthand some of the raptors cared for by the Bird TLC volunteers in their rustic facility.

On that January day, our breath froze in white clouds as we moved through the wooden hallways of the main building toward the outdoor enclosures. When we finally stepped into a snow-packed pen, I found myself gazing at a rather small and ragged-looking bald eagle perched on a log. Moving toward us, he spread out a single graceful wing, balancing his steps as he came. I realized then that this was the bird called One Wing. I had heard his amazing story but was not prepared for his intense presence. Here was a creature who was not only a survivor, but an inspiration and symbol of hope to all who had been in contact with him during his recovery. The experience of that day would stay with me, and the seed planted by that visit would grow into a series of drawings. The drawings in turn would beg to have their stories told, resulting in this book.

My goal in creating this book was to capture, in some small way, the individuality of these birds, yet I find the artist's hand falls short of mirroring their unique beauty. Words, too, seem inadequate. Many qualities usually associated with humans seem to be embodied in the birds, including courage, joy, loyalty, and determination. Nevertheless, my natural inclination to attribute such emotions and personality traits to these fascinating creatures is not based on scientific theories or studies. It is merely my personal interpretation of their behavior.

One Wing's Gift, in the end, is a tribute to the remarkable wild birds that have been cared for by the generous volunteers of Bird TLC. There are many such bird rescue centers throughout the United States and the world. They all provide opportunities for injured birds to be rehabilitated and returned to the wild whenever possible. Volunteers are always welcome. Please inquire in your local area should you wish to become trained as a caretaker or assist in the educational efforts of an avian rescue group. You will find that the rewards are abundant.

One Wing

BALD EAGLE

For three days the small bald eagle eluded the rescue workers trying to run him down. The blackened, oiled birds he was consuming for sustenance were sluggish and simple to scavenge. But eventually, flying became impossible for the eagle as the toxins from his prey spread throughout his body. In desperate attempts to become airborne, he injured himself against the rocks again and again; in the end, amputation would be the only option for his mangled left wing.

In the spring of 1989, following the *Exxon Valdez* oil spill in Prince William Sound, Dr. Jim Scott's Arctic Animal Hospital in Anchorage became a "MASH" center where the most badly injured bald eagles were brought for treatment. When One Wing arrived, no one thought his chances were very good. There were many sick eagles to be treated; toxins in their oiled prey had poisoned them. Only transfusions of eagle blood could give them any hope, and Dr. Scott had to select one of these birds as a blood donor since there were no healthy bald eagles to use for this purpose. Dr. Scott chose One Wing because he would never be able to fly again or be returned to the wild. His chances of surviving at all were very poor.

Normally, blood for a transfusion can be taken from an eagle no more often than every two weeks. Now it was drawn from One Wing each day for three days in a row, followed by one day of rest. More blood was taken for several additional days in succession. One Wing should never have survived, but each morning he was still alive when the weary vet arrived to check on his charges. Gazing back quietly from his cage, the eagle was clinging to life. Everyone in the clinic was amazed at One Wing's valiant fight to live; a small miracle was unfolding before them.

Corbie

Ironically, Corbie's life was saved by the *Exxon Valdez* oil spill. A clean-up worker spotted her floundering on a beach one morning, her wing broken by a fall from her nest. Without human activity along the oiled coastline, she would have undoubtedly perished. A baby northwestern crow has blue eyes when it is young, and the inside of its beak is red. Corbie's eyes had already changed to the dark brown of an adult, her mouth the characteristic black.

As a crow, Corbie is a member of the highly social Corvid family, which also includes ravens, magpies, and jays. Corvids are considered to be among the most intelligent of birds, displaying great adaptability and creativity. There are documented cases of crows using twigs for tools and also dropping clamshells while in flight, to expose the tasty meal inside.

Alex Carter, Corbie's first caretaker, kept her roomy cage in his home office. He wanted to interact with her as much as possible. Corbie would soon become a teaching bird, and this familiarity would help them both during presentations. Her cage door was left open so Corbie would feel less confined, and she began making frequent reconnaissance trips throughout the room. Rustling her feathers noisily in anticipation, she found the tile floor easily reachable with one graceful hop. Quickly tapping across the floor, dipping her head rhythmically, the young crow missed nothing with her darting, jet black eyes. This was an activity she especially relished when left home alone.

One day, Alex returned home from work to find fifty stone arrowheads neatly arrayed on his office floor in a semicircle. All of them belonged to a collection housed in a basket on a low bookshelf. Each one appeared to have been carefully placed and oriented in a vertical position. Alex knew that neither he nor his wife had taken the arrowheads out of the basket, and as he was gathering them up, he noticed he was under the dark, attentive eyes of the resident crow. The next day, when he went into the room, he found the same semicircular arrangement. Other arrowheads were scattered about the room as well, including under the closet door and on top of the baseboard heater. After several weeks of this game, Alex finally had to move the basket out of "beak reach."

Since then, Corbie has moved to caretaker Wayne Rush's house, and she has begun her teaching forays in earnest. Comfortable and safe on Wayne's gloved hand, she bobs and bows gracefully before her audience, fourteen ounces of mischievousness. Her intense eyes dart from person to person, but her gaze returns most often to Wayne. She seems to be in perpetual motion, alternately fluffing or smoothing her dark, iridescent feathers. When she stretches her wings, preening and caressing them, the stiff shafts click audibly back into place. In the springtime, Corbie's feathers fluff out and hang loosely on her flanks. She also develops a brood patch. This is a warm spot of bare skin, and Corbie would use it together with her downy feathers to cover her eggs and line a nest if she were free.

Corbie has never imitated human noises, as some crows are known to do. Instead she makes a distinctive crow sound that resembles the sound of a cork being pulled out of a bottle. She also mimics the spaniel, Sunday, who lives with her. She still loves venturing out of her cage to explore, and she delights in stealing its door fasteners and spiriting them away. Sometimes they are never found again. Corbie's favorite plaything is a bowl of brightly colored glass beads. She also takes pleasure in moving magnetic letters around on a metal cookie sheet. Wayne provides these things specifically to interest and amuse her.

Raids on the cat bowl allow Corbie to make away with the star-shaped food, which she stores in her throat pouch to be played with or eaten later. This pouch is a great advantage to crows when caching food in the wild. They have been observed gathering food on beaches while the tide is out and making quick trips to the shoreline to deposit their finds temporarily. This way, they can spend as much time as possible feeding and be able to gather larger quantities for themselves and their young.

Corbie is expected to have many years of life ahead of her. Crows have been known to live more than sixteen years in captivity. Throughout that time she will continue to playfully enlighten humans about the surprising intricacies of crow behavior.

NORTHWESTERN CROW (*Corvus caurinus*)
Size: 14 to 17 inches long; 34-inch wingspan.
Identifying characteristics: Squared-off tail, slightly smaller than common crow.
Plumage: Entirely black, with a strong metallic gloss.
Diet: Shellfish, insects, dead fish and mammals, and refuse.
Range: Restricted to coastal areas from Alaska to Washington.
Habitat: Ocean beaches, coastal villages, and cities.
Nesting habits: Builds a well-constructed stick nest in trees; nests in colonies.
Clutch size: Typically 4 to 5 eggs; incubation time of 16 to 21 days.
Voice: Low-pitched and hoarse: *kaah-kaah-kaah.*

Chitina

NORTHERN HARRIER

Mary Bethe Wright will never forget the time she took Chitina out for an educational presentation on a tour boat. The request to speak on board with the northern harrier had been enticing. They were to sail across Prince William Sound, a trip from Valdez to Whittier that is breathtaking in its beauty. But the frigid waters of the Sound can be fickle, and the weather turned bad that day. The wind came up without warning, sending seasick passengers hastily to the railings as their boat tossed on the waves.

Mary Bethe and Chitina were faring no better. The small, gray-blue hawk had patiently spent several hours on the glove as his caretaker shared her knowledge and answered questions. Hunkering down now on her arm—something he had never done in the five years they had worked together—he looked at her with forlorn golden eyes. Sensing his distress, Mary Bethe crouched down and placed him on the deck. As the seas calmed some, they worked their way over to his open cage and a safe haven for the unhappy bird. Northern harriers, it seems, are landlubbers.

Chitina was found close to the town in Alaska for which he was named. His wing crushed, amputation seemed likely when he arrived at the Bird TLC clinic. Yet Dr. Scott decided against it, knowing it might one day give limited use. Even after healing, though, the harrier's wing never lost its characteristic droop. But Chitina would remain whole, though the experience of flying and hunting would not be his again.

One of the first teaching birds at Bird TLC, Chitina "trained" many of the presenters currently working in the program. Although he weighed just over sixteen ounces, he was technically difficult to handle. Certain procedures had to be followed when putting him into his cage or taking him out. Alex Carter, his first caretaker, laughs softly when recalling Chitina's temperament. If you rushed the harrier, he would realize it, and all cooperation ceased.

Northern harriers live in moist, marshy areas by preference. Their long, slender legs are adapted perfectly for a wet environment. Eating the smaller birds, rodents, and frogs that live in such areas, these hawks literally "harry" their prey with long, slow flights, weaving back and forth.

Wild northern harriers have surprising nesting rituals. Built on the ground, their nests could conceivably be very vulnerable to predators. But the female, who sits alone on her eggs, protects her nest with great ferocity. She even forbids her mate to approach, which creates a predicament when he arrives with food. The solution involves a delicate and enchanting dance above the nest. Circling low, the male signals that he has brought a mouse or other tidbit. The female responds by flying up to meet him, turning upside-down at the moment when they touch, and receiving the morsel from him in midair.

This trait may explain some of Chitina's habits in captivity. One time, Mary Bethe agreed to give Chitina dinner when Alex was away. She put the hungry harrier in his enclosure and placed at his feet a meal of small white mice, defrosted and ready to eat. A short while later, she walked back by the bird and noticed there was a mouse in his beak, its tail hanging from one side. Chitina immediately gave her a sharp look that said unmistakably, "You aren't welcome right now! Please go away!" When she remained, looking on with curiosity, Chitina began to cackle. Plainly, he desired no audience at suppertime. Alex later admitted he was never allowed to observe the hawk eating dinner either.

Some teaching birds thrive on stroking and tactile interaction with their handlers. Chitina, however, disliked being touched as a rule, and Mary Bethe always respected that. She firmly believes that this respect is what allowed them to get along so well. Sometimes she would lightly run her finger over Chitina's breastbone, or "keel." Chitina didn't object to this classic way of gauging a bird's weight, but his sleek, bluish feathers were his alone to preen and care for.

Mary Bethe talks fondly of Chitina and their years together in the educational program with Bird TLC. Both she and Alex refer to him as a teacher. His dignity and pride made him unforgettable, laced as they were with a fussy, temperamental nature. Regardless of the caretaker or the type of bird, it is clear that the relationships that form at the clinic always radiate with devotion and respect.

NORTHERN HARRIER (Circus cyaneus)
   Size: 16.5 inches long; 42-inch wingspan.
   Identifying characteristics: Medium-size hawk, long wings and tail, white rump.
   Plumage: Male is blue-gray; female is dark brown with buff underparts.
   Diet: Small mammals, reptiles, amphibians, birds.
   Range: Alaska and Canada in summer; ranges to South America in winter.
   Habitat: Grasslands and marshes.
   Nesting habits: Ground nester.
   Clutch size: Typically 4 to 6 eggs; incubation time of 31 to 32 days.
   Voice: A series of about 10 short, sharp whistles.

Grumpy

GREAT HORNED OWL

Perhaps "Grumpess" should have been his name, but no one ever knew his gender for sure. "Grumpy" was easier for the volunteers to say, and the name seemed to fit his countenance, punctuated as it was with feathered, frowning eyebrows. He had come to the Bird TLC clinic with a gunshot wound that ultimately robbed him of his left wing. Great horned owls are imposing birds, even when they are not physically whole, but this one's huge yellow eyes were his most unforgettable feature. Grumpy's gaze was always intense and piercing; he missed nothing in his vicinity.

After Grumpy healed, the clinic became his residence. But, for the great bird, a void remained that could not be filled in captivity. A sense of despondency seemed to overcome him before many months had passed. Taking pity on the owl, Barbara Doak brought him to her home in Anchorage to live. One of the original volunteers for Bird TLC, Barbara provided a safe, permanent haven for several feathered residents.

Being a nocturnal creature, Grumpy moved about very little during the day. With this relative inactivity, he saved energy for his solitary nighttime hours. People who slept in the rooms next to his cage reported that he bounced around all night long. A series of deeply resonant *hoooo* notes announced his pleasure while bathing in the quiet darkness. Morning light illuminated a soggy floor and cage, but its untidy state was of no particular concern to Grumpy. Great horned owls have casual housekeeping habits in the wild, occasionally accumulating so many dead animals in the nest that their young succumb to disease.

Silent and motionless most of the time, Grumpy was a stately, dignified presence in the house. The owl was acutely aware of everything occurring in his domain. When outside his cage, he watched all that happened both in the backyard and through the skylight in the sunroom where he resided. He peered through the adjacent living room window for a view of that side of his world. One could follow the mail carrier's approach just by watching the movements of Grumpy's head. Owls are able to rotate their heads about three-quarters of a full circle to look around them, compensating for not being able to turn their eyes in their sockets. Many wild animals are uncomfortable being looked at directly, but Grumpy was a master at staring people down.

An incredible sense of hearing also aided him in this self-appointed household surveillance. Special adaptations allow owls to pinpoint noises even without using their acute vision. Fleshy ear flaps funneled and concentrated sounds, and differently shaped right and left ear openings combined to assist Grumpy in precisely locating barking dogs or approaching visitors with equal ease.

Normally Grumpy's privacy was very important to him—he wanted no one watching when he ate or produced his pellet. The pellet is not excrement, but an odorless packaging of fur and bones—the indigestible parts of food (white mice, in Grumpy's case), neatly compacted and coughed up daily by owls.

If his routine was disturbed, Grumpy communicated his displeasure in colorful ways. Once, an African gray parrot named Harry was staying in the house while his owner was away. Harry was most vocal, which clearly vexed Grumpy. Finally, the owl had simply had enough; he stalked to the end of his perch and expelled his pellet out onto the computer where Barbara was working. Another time, when a stranger cleaned his cage, Grumpy left a similar deposit smack on the person's head.

Nearly fourteen years after he first arrived at Bird TLC, Grumpy fell ill with symptoms of advanced age. While he was sick, he had to be force-fed his diet of mice, a process he clearly hated. Another volunteer offered to do the feeding so that Barbara could preserve the owl's trust. Each time the volunteer arrived, Grumpy knew with certainty why she was there and tried desperately to escape using his one remaining wing. Eventually he recovered enough to eat mice on his own once again, and the volunteer went away. But, several months later when the same volunteer came to visit, Grumpy remembered her. Those intense yellow eyes watched her with wary distrust during her entire stay.

As one of the original teaching birds for Bird TLC, Grumpy made more trips to classrooms and groups than anyone could count. All those who knew this owl were struck by his dignity, and his presence still looms in their memory.

GREAT HORNED OWL (*Bubo virginianus*)
Size: 20 inches long; 55-inch wingspan.
Identifying characteristics: Large owl with prominent ear tufts, yellow eyes.
Plumage: Mottled brown upper parts, pale underparts, white throat patch.
Diet: Small mammals, reptiles, amphibians, birds.
Range: Common from Alaska to the southern tip of South America.
Habitat: Most often forests, but can inhabit mountains, marshes, or deserts.
Nesting habits: Frequently uses old nests of other birds of prey.
Clutch size: Typically 1 to 4 eggs; incubation time of 26 to 35 days.
Voice: A series of deep, resonant *hooo* notes, usually in sets of 5 or 8.

Blue

STELLER'S JAY

"Got by dog." The veterinarian had scribbled those words on the nestling's chart that June morning. The small Steller's jay he held in his hands had been mauled by a backyard pet. The most obvious injury, which would prevent the jay from ever being returned to the wild, was a compound fracture of the left wing that left the bone protruding from the skin. There were also head lacerations and leg injuries. But it could have been worse: had the wounds come from a cat's teeth, the bacteria in its saliva would have caused a dangerous infection within hours.

This was clearly a bird that would need constant attention to survive. Volunteering at Bird TLC that morning, Barbara Doak willingly assumed round-the-clock care of the jay. She decided to call him Blue. At the end of the day, she bundled the fledgling into a small cardboard box for the trip home. The red "wing wrap" covering the tiny bird was made of material similar to that used on human burn victims; it would help his injuries to heal. Blue looked like a broken Christmas ornament. Stroking his matted down, Barbara wondered if he would pull through.

That evening, Blue stubbornly refused to open his beak at feeding time. When Barbara tenderly pried it open, Blue responded by vigorously shaking his head and voicing his protest. But, after swallowing a bite or two, he began licking his chops with a long, mobile tongue. Strengthened by the nourishment, he finally began preening his cobalt feathers. Obviously, Blue was quite hungry; yet he still would not willingly eat. Careful examination revealed the reason: a jagged crack ran halfway across his lower beak.

The next day, back at the clinic, Dr. Scott provided an ingenious solution to the problem. Taking a piece of quill from an eagle feather, he slathered epoxy liberally along its hollow length. Then, cupping the squirming jay in his hands, he skillfully positioned the unusual splint in place over the broken beak. Just as delicate were the long five minutes that followed, as he held the indignant bird still while the glue dried.

The fix held. From then on, Blue's recovery was rapid and joyful. By the evening feeding he was behaving like a proper baby jay. Crouching and fluttering his wings, he gobbled food from a child's watercolor paintbrush in between noisy hunger cries.

Blue's improving health allowed trips to the greenhouse in Barbara's backyard to search for bugs and worms. Left to his own devices, he would be an independent character for a while. Then, suddenly, he would begin screeching loudly for "mom" and would listen for reassurance that Barbara was near before returning to his explorations. Almost like a puppy, he followed her about the house, down the basement stairs, and even into the shower.

The months passed, and Blue matured into a handsome and mischievous bird. While he learned about Barbara's home, now his permanent residence, she learned about jay-proofing it. Every plant was wrapped with protective wire, no jar remained uncovered, and cupboards were filled with items formerly left on the counter. Caching became Blue's predominant activity, and anything was fair game. He stored peanuts under the rug and stuffed paper clips in with the plants. Barbara's hearing aid ended up in the mealworm tank.

By accident, Barbara discovered Blue's favorite treat. One evening she was struggling to spear the last few olives from a tall, narrow jar. Just as a round, green orb bobbed to the top, Blue materialized and made a desperate stab at it. When Barbara let him take one, Blue carefully cached the olive in a garden work glove, saving his treasure for a future snack.

Several years have passed since Blue first came to live with humans. Today, he is a vivacious adult Steller's jay, still filled with insatiable curiosity. The trusty eagle-quill splint that saved his life grew off long ago. In a special glass view cage, he makes forays to classrooms or meetings for educational presentations. At home with Barbara, Blue is usually out of his enclosure and busy doing whatever comes naturally to a jay living in a house.

Barbara watches Blue's antics with a quiet smile. By not attempting to train or control him, she is able to take great pleasure in discovering new aspects of his jay-ness. Perhaps Blue is teaching tolerance of idiosyncrasies. Possibly his message is "live and let live." But Barbara feels much wiser for having shared her life with him.

STELLER'S JAY (Cyanocitta stelleri)
Size: 11 inches long; 19-inch wingspan.
Identifying characteristics: Sturdy black bill, black crest, short rounded wings.
Plumage: Dusky head and body, blue wings and tail.
Diet: Mostly nuts, fruits, and seeds, lesser quantities of insects.
Range: Alaska, California coast, Rocky Mountains, Central America.
Habitat: Prefers coniferous forests.
Nesting habits: Builds a bulky open cup of twigs with a lining of grass or hair.
Clutch size: Typically 3 to 5 eggs; incubation time of 16 days.
Voice: Low-pitched, raucous, and varied; imitates hawks perfectly.

Little Babe

YELLOW WARBLER

Though Little Babe was a tiny bird, barely a finger's length in size, her personality far outstretched her minute dimensions. She was nearly dead when she reached Bird TLC as one of four yellow warbler hatchlings that had spilled from their tree during a windstorm. Delicate transparent bodies and oversized heads looked as though they were sprinkled with dandelion down. Caregivers gently placed the small birds in a scrubbed, cotton-lined margarine container. Because towels could easily snag the birds' miniscule nails and injure their toes and feet, they nestled together atop a white tissue coverlet. Only a few days old, the chicks relied on the warmth from a heating pad tucked under the plastic laundry basket that held their makeshift dwelling. Sensing they were in a nest again, the little birds instinctively helped with housekeeping. Even at this tender age, they wobbled to the rim to excrete their waste.

Sadly, two died almost at once, but the remaining two seemed to thrive and grow stronger with care and special baby-bird food. A strange mixture, it contained such unlikely ingredients as monkey chow and canned dog food, along with bone meal and vitamins. Hatchlings possess ravenous appetites, and already these were "gaping"— opening their mouths wide and begging for food. Little Babe and her sibling greedily accepted the oatmeal-like gruel, daubed inside their beaks with a watercolor paintbrush.

Within a week, both babies began to hop about, exploring their new world. Beyond the age of fifteen days, most young birds prefer to sit on branches, even though they are still quite clumsy. With wide-open eyes and tiny pinfeathers to preen, these two had arrived at the "brancher" stage of life. Fluttering their wings with expectation, they watched for the paintbrush spoons. Then, without any warning, the small warblers grew weaker and were unable to stay on a perch. They lay listlessly in the bottom of their cage except when they were picked up to be fed.

Trying to find out what could have gone wrong, concerned volunteers discovered that a new kind of bone meal was being used at the clinic that spring. Because it didn't contain the proper proportions of calcium and phosphorus, the tiny creatures were unable to thrive. Though the formula was immediately adjusted, the weakest baby warbler soon died. Little Babe, however, gained strength and perched again within twelve hours. Mealworms rolled in bone meal were prepared for her, and she greedily accepted them from helping fingers.

When her strength returned, Little Babe moved in with Barbara Doak. She shared her home with Rocky, a large rottweiler dog; the very social Steller's jay named Blue; and Grumpy, the one-winged great horned owl. A mere four inches long, the diminutive warbler displayed more muted plumage than the vibrant yellow feathers common to the female of her species. A tiny tuft of white splashed her head, a unique decoration all her own. From the beginning, Little Babe was incredibly tame. Soon given free run of the sunroom, she delighted in snacking on the lavender blossoms that grew there. Sometimes we don't think of tiny birds as having unique personalities, but there was no question that this particular one was quite gregarious, outgoing, and loving.

Little Babe was especially playful. She would sneak up on Rocky while he was asleep and peck him on the nose before making a quick getaway. Blue wasn't safe from her pranks either, and the little warbler often entered his cage just to tease him. Little Babe was also tiny enough to squeeze through the bars of Grumpy's cage and alight on the far end of his perch, eyeing him all the while. Fortunately, the owl was too slow to do much about this insolent baiting. He ignored the intruder in his dignified manner.

But Barbara was her great love. The small warbler preferred staying close to her, although she learned to fly with elegant skill and could easily have remained more aloof and independent. Alighting on one shoulder, Little Babe would dispense kisses, gently exploring Barbara's cheek and lips with her tiny beak. She had become too used to humans, and too tame, to survive in the wild. All fear was lost, and gone with it was her chance to be free. In Barbara's house she lived out her life, a sweet source of pleasure to everyone who had the good fortune to know her. For Barbara, Little Babe was a special creature she would never forget.

YELLOW WARBLER (Dendroica petechia)
Size: 4 inches long; 7.25-inch wingspan.
Identifying characteristics: Small, active bird; thin-pointed bill, yellowish legs.
Plumage: Male is mostly yellow with rusty streaks on breast; female is yellow.
Diet: Almost exclusively insects, lesser quantities of fruit.
Range: Alaska, Canada, continental United States, South America.
Habitat: Common in willow thickets, orchards, and suburban shrubbery.
Nesting habits: Builds a well-constructed cup nest; may build a second story.
Clutch size: Typically 3 to 6 eggs; incubation time of 11 to 12 days.
Voice: About 7 clear, sweet notes: *sweet-sweet-sweet-setta-see-see-whew.*

Healy

GOLDEN EAGLE

Golden eagles are among the largest aerial predators in the world. They are true pursuers of prey, in contrast to the more opportunistic bald eagles. But hunting is a skill that Healy never learned, for reasons known only to him. Already a mature bird, Healy was discovered close to Denali Park in early summer, just north of the town for which he was named. Starving and underweight, he was so weak he couldn't fly.

A veterinarian in Fairbanks stabilized the eagle. He carefully ran his hands over Healy's golden-brown feathers, gently exploring the wings and legs of the gaunt creature. Satisfied that there were no injuries or abnormalities, he began an aggressive feeding regimen to restore the bird's strength and weight. Quail turned out to be Healy's favorite delicacy. He accepted them with great relish.

After a few weeks the eagle was placed with a falconer in the area to try sharpening his hunting skills. But it became apparent before very long that he had no interest in catching his own prey. Puzzled, the falconer could only speculate that Healy may have been raised in captivity. His uncharacteristically calm demeanor seemed to suggest this as well. Soon, everyone realized that Healy would never be able to be free again. Bird TLC offered one possibility for providing a lifetime home.

There was no hesitation on Alex Carter's part when he learned of Healy's plight. Having had experience in the Rocky Mountains with raptors, he had a special place in his heart for golden eagles. With wood and wire he fashioned a comfortable enclosure, called a "mew" by falconers, in his yard. So Healy came at last to a place that would be a permanent and loving residence.

Golden eagles evolved earlier in time than their distant cousins, the bald eagles. They are named for the rich gold coloration of the feathers adorning their heads. A close inspection of the brown plumage on the wings and body reveals that gold tinges linger there as well. Belonging to the family of booted eagles, goldens have feathers reaching clear to their feet. These creatures are magnificent to behold.

Now a mature eagle weighing more than eleven pounds, Healy is heavy on the glove. When you see him with Alex, the first thing that strikes you is the sheer size of this bird. The intelligent amber eyes are riveting, the beak gracefully curved and powerful. But the eagle's feet are clearly the "business end" of this raptor. The talons appear oversized, even for such a massive body. A falconer can suffer a broken arm when a golden eagle accidentally lands too roughly, but Healy demonstrates exceptional restraint with his human companion. Keeping the strength of his talons carefully in check, he shifts his weight with ease on Alex's gloved hand.

The trust and friendship between this noble eagle and the man who cares for him shine through the body language of the two when they're together. Ruffling his feathers comfortably, Healy leans close and arches his head over Alex's. In a gesture resembling an affectionate hug, Alex softly brushes his cheek against Healy's feathers.

Outside for daily exercise sessions, Alex and Healy often engage in play. Tapping the eagle's breast and legs gently with a small twig, Alex invites a game of tug. Accepting, Healy grabs away the stick and makes off with it. A long tether, securely fastened to his leg band, allows the eagle ample space to roam Alex's expansive lawn in safety. Healy has also been known to edge over to the garden and assist in the weeding. Ripping up plugs of grass, he follows Alex along the rows of vegetables in a very un-eagle-like pastime. In the summer he occasionally enjoys spray from a hose; fluffing up his feathers with pleasure, he utters low cries. All of Healy's sounds are muted and melodious. These predatory birds have no need for noisy calls to alert prey to their presence.

The hours spent with Alex building trust have allowed Healy to be comfortable and safe in educational presentations. In a classroom full of wide-eyed children, Alex has no doubt that the eagle will be a calm ambassador. Healy models peace, loyalty, and gentle strength. A soft-spoken, unassuming man, Alex makes light of the huge investment of time and energy required to care for the stately bird. "Without a doubt, this work has given me more than I ever give back," he says, his heartfelt words a tribute to their relationship.

GOLDEN EAGLE (Aquila chrysaetos)
   Size: 32 inches long; 78-inch wingspan.
   Identifying characteristics: Broad-winged, legs feathered to toes, dark beak.
   Plumage: Almost entirely brown, golden feathering on nape and head.
   Diet: Mostly small mammals; also birds, reptiles, amphibians.
   Range: Alaska, Canada, continental United States, and South America.
   Habitat: Forests, mountains, tundra, temperate highland areas.
   Nesting habits: Builds a huge nest on cliffs overlooking its hunting grounds.
   Clutch size: Typically 1 to 3 eggs; incubation time of 43 to 45 days.
   Voice: Rapid, sharp chirps.

Carroll

BALD EAGLE

The frozen mice that she wanted lay high atop a platform in her cage. Bob Collins, her keeper, had placed them there. If she was to eat supper, she would have to climb up the series of perches he had fashioned. Not only that, but she would have to pump her wings to assist her in the task. The huge bald eagle glared at the man, but she had grown accustomed to his presence in her enclosure. She could sense the food, and her hunger was growing. Unfolding her great wings a bit as if to practice, she beat the air with unsure strokes. Then she began a reluctant climb to the top.

Several months earlier, Dr. Scott had asked Bob, a local falconer, if he might be able to train the young female as a teaching bird. At fourteen pounds, she was powerful and difficult to handle. A collision injury had damaged the joint in one of her wings, and now the wing had stiffened, hanging limply at her side. It was painful to use, and she simply chose to avoid that discomfort.

When she had been healthy, she had flown with the deep, powerful strokes characteristic of her kind, soaring effortlessly on outspread wings. Highly territorial, these raptors spend much of their time waiting patiently for fish to surface on lakes or streams. The sight of a mature bald eagle swooping to the water with a graceful swiftness, spread talons already reaching in anticipation, is not soon forgotten.

Having watched the magnificent bird all those weeks, Bob began to wonder whether she was as crippled as everyone thought. He could see that using the wing was uncomfortable for her. But he also realized she needed to exercise it if she had any hope of regaining flight.

It was a painstaking process. The eagle had not wished to use her wing again, but now she had no choice if she wanted her food. And so she reluctantly accepted this daily feeding ritual that would continue into the weeks ahead. Slowly the ligaments and muscles in her wing grew stronger. After a few more months of this food-fetching exercise, it was time to move her from the clinic in Anchorage to a larger pen.

The Bird TLC flight center is located at Fort Richardson, tucked away in a remote area called Camp Carroll. Built from scratch after the *Exxon Valdez* spill, the center now offered a better situation for the eagle. Extending from a narrow building that holds the separate indoor enclosures, the flight pens are constructed of plywood and sturdy wire. The spacious interior of these open-air pens allows recuperating raptors ample room to exercise. Each is about ninety feet by thirty feet, with a ceiling height of twenty feet. Five separate pens can each accommodate several birds at any one time. This is where Bob now moved the large eagle, hoping she might be encouraged to practice flying once again. Up to this time, Bob had never referred to her by a name. Now it seemed to him that "Carroll" might be just right, the name of the location where she could relearn her skills.

The next evening, Bob carefully opened the whitewashed wooden door to the eagle's outside pen, not knowing where she would be resting. A quick glance around showed no trace of her. Striding to the opposite end, Bob peered behind a pile of stumps that served as perches, but she was still nowhere to be seen. Absently he glanced upward, and there she was. Perched with confidence on a high bar, Carroll was gazing back at her familiar caretaker. An instant later, she leapt into the air, swooping easily along the length of pen. She was flying again and proud of it.

A group of Bird TLC volunteers gathered for Carroll's release a few weeks later, after her consummate aerial skills had been regained in full. It had taken a year to bring her that far. Bob had willingly invested two hours a day without fail, coaxing and cajoling, never losing patience. He smiles as he remembers the day of her release and how he watched the great bird soar away until she was only a speck in the morning sky. Out loud he called "Goodbye" and wished her luck. Then softly, under his breath, he added, "Doggone it—I knew you could do it!"

BALD EAGLE *(Haliaeetus leucocephalus)*
Size: 30 to 43 inches long; 78- to 96-inch wingspan.
Identifying characteristics: Broad rounded wings, broad tail, thick hooked bill.
Plumage: White head and neck, white tail, dark brown body plumage, yellow bill.
Diet: Fish, either alive or dead, small mammals, birds.
Range: Alaska and Canada in summer; continental United States in winter.
Habitat: Ocean shorelines or rivers, wetlands.
Nesting habits: Builds a huge platform nest, up to 12 feet high, called an eyrie.
Clutch size: Typically 2 eggs; incubation time of 34 to 36 days.
Voice: Similar to rapid, sharp chirps of golden eagle, but softer: *kuh-kuh-kuh.*

Ravenhood

COMMON RAVEN

She had trapped and killed the unwary mouse in her pen, flipping it over quickly and disabling its legs to prevent it from darting away. This was purely instinctual, since Ravenhood had never known a teacher with feathers or a bill. The rodent remained clenched in her strong, black beak; she would refrain from feasting until her caretaker arrived. Then she would dismember her furry prize, offering him the choicest parts.

A special bond exists between this exquisitely dark and glossy raven and her caretaker, Colin Matthews. Merriment infuses their communication. The noises are metallic, loud, and melodious. Ravenhood has a repertoire of about fifteen sounds, but a wild cousin would know around twenty-five. Colin himself is well versed in raven language and encourages her, murmuring *huck-a-choo, huck-a-chooie,* and *knock knock knock.* The knocking sounds express affection, and all of the raven's utterings have different meanings, some known only to her.

The bird's body language, though, is unmistakable. Bobbing, dipping her head, and raising her head feathers straight up, Ravenhood mischievously leans toward Colin. She waits to be rubbed and scratched, luxuriating in the attention. With complete trust, she rubs her head on Colin's hand, nuzzling affectionately against his skin. Opening her beak, she invites him to rub the inside of her mouth and stroke her velvety tongue.

Ravenhood, also known as "Hood," was discovered after falling from her nest. Born with a birth defect that prevented her left wing from ever extending fully, she could not sustain flight. Most likely Hood had been on her maiden excursion when she fell: her mouth was still the red of a baby raven and her eyes were still blue. The dirty gray of her plumage contrasted with the vibrant black of an adult. Had she not been discovered, she surely would have perished. Under Colin's care, Hood grew to her present weight of two pounds and blossomed into a beautiful, healthy bird.

To see a raven close-up is a rare treat. The sheen of Hood's feathers is almost mirror-like. It's also hard to keep your eyes from Ravenhood's beak. Colin compares it to a pair of needle-nose pliers. Long and powerful, it can easily snap a good-size stick or serve as a formidable weapon. Yet she can just as easily hold a fragile chicken egg until she is ready to open it, delicately consuming the yolk and discarding the white. The gentleness Hood displays when playing with her human companion is all the more amazing because of the purposeful restraint she uses.

Hood's feet and legs are likewise enthralling to watch. Constantly in motion, it seems, they are encircled by her jesses. The long, kangaroo-leather thongs were fastened there in babyhood, and Hood seems to consider them an extension of her feet. They allow Colin to secure her to his gloved fist during her excursions as a teaching bird. Fussing with them from time to time, Hood straightens them out fastidiously in front of her, arranging them to her liking.

Play is the paramount activity in any raven's day. Whether hanging upside-down for fun or rolling in her water tub like a rambunctious puppy, Hood simply radiates joy. In the wild, ravens will slide down snowy slopes on their backs for the sheer delight of it. Hood is not above lying on her back, either. A soup bone hung as a toy in her enclosure for quite some time but eventually fell to the ground. The raven attacked it ferociously, holding it to her breast with her feet and beak while on her back, exacting revenge by flipping it into the air again and again. Hood also loves to "play catch" with small objects. Ping-pong balls are a special favorite, and the energetic raven bounces them back to Colin, using her beak with practiced skill. Her speed is dizzying.

As a teaching bird, Ravenhood is without peer for her species. When the dog kennel she travels in appears, her excitement bubbles over. She's always ready to go. Her outgoing personality and willingness to vocalize for groups of youngsters or adults is unique. Colin describes her as a "gutsy bird." The mutual trust and love he shares with Hood are obvious. This species has been known to live thirty years in captivity. In the company of a good friend like Colin, Ravenhood should enjoy a long life.

COMMON RAVEN *(Corvus corax)*

Size: 21 to 27 inches long; 53-inch wingspan.

Identifying characteristics: Wedge-shaped tail, short dark legs, heavy black bill.

Plumage: Entirely black.

Diet: Primarily carrion, lesser quantities of reptiles, eggs, insects, and plants.

Range: Arctic and far north regions, western United States, Appalachia.

Habitat: Tidal flats, ocean beaches, old-growth forests, mountains, urban areas.

Nesting habits: Builds a stick nest up to 30 inches wide with a soft, deep lining.

Clutch size: Typically 3 to 7 eggs; incubation time of 18 to 21 days.

Voice: Commonly low, hoarse croaks; capable of vocalizing many sounds.

Valentine

GYRFALCON

It seemed unbelievable, but there she was. Following behind two ranch hands, almost like a stray dog, was an aged falcon. Her luminous black eyes tracked their every movement as she trudged along after them. Awkwardly picking her way across the ground with widespread talons better suited to gripping branches, she was in trouble. Far out in the pastures, the men had been busying themselves with the many chores that come with spring in Nebraska. Neither of them had any idea that starvation had robbed the gyrfalcon of flight or that she was near death. But sensing that she needed help, they gently scooped her up with an old blanket. She put up no resistance. One of the men carried her on horseback, like a sleeping child, to the nearby town of Valentine.

Once the local veterinarian stabilized and fed the hungry bird, she was sent to the University of Minnesota's raptor facility for rehabilitation. Happily, plenty of food and rest proved to be the only medicine she required to heal. By the end of that summer she was healthy again, and plans were made for her release back to the wild.

Gyrfalcons are the only birds of prey that remain in the Arctic year-round. They even stay close to nesting areas in the winter if enough prey is available to them. It seemed logical to return the bird to the breeding grounds in Alaska. Late that August, Dr. Jim Scott got a call asking if Bird TLC would be willing to receive a rescued gyr (the common nickname for gyrfalcons, pronounced *jeer*). When she arrived at the airport, fall was already well under way. The birch and aspen were dressed in vibrant golds, and there was a bite in the air foretelling the fast-coming winter. Arrangements were made to have local falconer Bob Collins check her out before her release.

Bob was well versed in the care of gyrfalcons. Experience with his own falconry birds and with other injured ones had taught him much about these large raptors. A close inspection of the new arrival revealed that she was deep into her winter molt, already missing eight of her tail feathers. Some species molt twice yearly, before and after reproduction, shedding their feathers in a very systematic way. Freeing her now, with the first snow less than a month away, would have been disastrous for the elderly gyr. So Bob settled her in for the winter among his falconry birds and named her Valentine, after the town where she was rescued. She sported the less common snowy white plumage of her species, contrasting sharply with the dark gray gyrfalcons that were her companions. Yet they readily accepted this pale newcomer without complaint, sharing the daily meals of frozen quail they all relished.

Finally, the following June, amidst joyous fanfare, Valentine was set free close to the Tangle Lakes Drainage in Alaska. As she left Bob's glove and tasted the freedom of flight once again, there were few dry eyes among those watching the graceful, wheeling gyrfalcon. She had entrusted a year of her life to many different people, starting with the Nebraska ranch hands who had come to her aid. All had offered caring and kindness, allowing this moment to become a reality. Yet Bob couldn't shake his nagging concern that this elderly raptor might not fare well.

Late the next year, a musher was guiding his team of huskies along a familiar trail near Mount Maclaren. Up ahead, he caught sight of a mature white gyrfalcon resting on a rocky knoll they were approaching. As a resident of the area, the man was well acquainted with gyrs. It was common to see them at a distance, circling lazily in the sky. Never had he seen one so close, though, or so seemingly unafraid. She was in beautiful shape. Stopping the team, the musher anchored his dogs safely before he attempted to approach the bird. Gazing back at him with large, dark eyes, she allowed him to come within four or five feet of her. For several minutes, each watched the other in silence. Then the falcon lifted effortlessly away, so close that the man could feel the wind from her wings. The experience was one he would never forget.

When the musher called Bird TLC in Anchorage to report the unusual encounter, his tale spread among the volunteers. When Bob heard the news, he chuckled with delight. He likes to think that the aging gyr made it after all.

GYRFALCON (Falco rusticolus)
   Size: 20 inches long; 48-inch wingspan (the largest falcon).
   Identifying characteristics: Dark eyes, notched beak, pointed wings.
   Plumage: Can be gray, black, or white.
   Diet: Mostly birds, some small mammals such as rodents and hares.
   Range: Arctic and subarctic regions; rarely migrates below Canada.
   Habitat: Rocky sea coasts or rivers with bluffs, mountains above timberline.
   Nesting habits: Usually nests on the bare rock of a cliff.
   Clutch size: Typically 2 to 6 eggs; incubation time of 34 to 36 days.
   Voice: Varies from a soft *e-chup* to a loud, rapid-fire *kekk-kekk-kekk-kekk-kekk.*

Jewel

MERLIN

The small falcon lay motionless, a shattered tail streaming fan-like behind her. Drowsy from the anesthesia, Jewel was scarcely aware of the sure hands that deftly sliced away all but an inch from each ruined feather. Using an age-old falconry technique called "imping," caretaker Wayne Rush began the meticulous work of building a replacement tail for the injured merlin.

An array of sleek, richly dappled tail feathers, collected from local falconry birds as they had molted, lay piled close to Jewel. Chocolate-hued and splashed with creamy bands, they were a perfect match for the mature female's own coloration. A replacement tail slowly began to take shape as Wayne arranged loose feathers, like pieces of a jigsaw puzzle, in proper order on the table.

Next Wayne turned to an assortment of bamboo slivers. He would slip each wooden needle snugly into a hollow feather shaft, seamlessly joining old to new. Then he would be ready to epoxy these ingenious substitutes to the stubby remnants of Jewel's own tail.

While holding each shaft carefully in place during the five minutes it took the adhesive to dry, Wayne ran his hand softly over Jewel's slim body. Weighing in at only nine ounces, the lightweight raptor was a force to be reckoned with. Merlins are exceedingly swift and deadly, easily capable of taking prey their own size. Skimming low and erratically over open meadows, they make lightning grabs for startled birds that burst out of hiding. Utterly fearless, these small, dashing falcons have no hesitation about high-speed pursuits into wooded areas to make a kill. Few birds can escape them in straightaway flight.

Using a calm, reassuring touch, Jewel's caretaker took this opportunity to smooth her ruffled plumage and explore the healing wound on her right wing. Caged life was not what Jewel longed for; she still had a fierce love of freedom. Once recovered from the anesthesia, she would not willingly consent to any ministrations.

A few weeks earlier, the merlin had been discovered in the Bristol Bay area of Alaska. A sharp-eyed child, boating down the Kvichak River with his family, spied her floundering on the bank. Brought down by a gunshot, the bird had made thrashing attempts to fly that had tattered her tail and further damaged her crippled right wing. She was at the mercy of predators and already suffering from hunger and dehydration. Human intervention was her only hope for survival. Weakened too much to protest, the merlin didn't struggle as the boy's father gathered her up in a spare parka and placed her carefully in his son's lap. This dark cocoon helped calm the frightened bird during the family's trip downriver.

A rescue flight from the village of Levelock carried the merlin to Bird TLC's clinic in Anchorage, where all was in readiness to treat the injured falcon. Surgery would take most of her mangled right wing, but her prospects for recovery were hopeful.

Not so certain was whether the merlin could ever learn to trust people or fully mend from the circumstances that tore her from the wild. Eye contact with humans often threw her into damaging frenzies, so she was kept away from bright lights and people and respectfully housed in a quiet corner. She began to accept physical contact as weeks of kind treatment slipped by, but a human gaze seemed to remain unbearable to her.

As the merlin healed, her need for a long-term home prompted a call to Wayne Rush. The investment of time required of a permanent caretaker is substantial and can span many years. When Wayne visited the clinic to have his first glimpse of the merlin, he had no illusions about the difficulty of the undertaking he had readily agreed to. Soon the falcon would move to his home and, with time, might assist with educational presentations for local school children.

Accompanied by his two young granddaughters, Olivia and Gracie, Wayne stepped carefully past tidy wire and wood enclosures containing a variety of wild birds in all stages of recovery. Reaching the merlin's cage, Olivia stood on tiptoe to glimpse inside. As Wayne bent down to scoop up Gracie, who was too small to peer in, he heard his older granddaughter gasp with delight. Looking with wonder into the falcon's huge, luminous eyes, the child stood spellbound for a long moment as the creature gazed calmly back without any hint of fear. Then, smiling widely, Olivia whispered, "Look, Papa! Her eyes are like jewels!" Little Gracie nodded in agreement, softly repeating the bird's new name as she stared in fascination.

MERLIN *(Falco columbarius)*
    Size: 12 inches long; 23-inch wingspan.
    Identifying characteristics: Long pointed wings; short, dark, hooked beak.
    Plumage: Male is dark blue-gray; female is dark brownish black.
    Diet: Almost exclusively birds; some small mammals and insects.
    Range: Alaska, Canada, continental United States.
    Habitat: A bird of open country—seashore, marshlands, short-grass steppes.
    Nesting habits: Typically nests in trees, utilizing abandoned nests.
    Clutch size: Typically 4 to 5 eggs; incubation time of 30 to 35 days.
    Voice: A series of high-pitched notes: *ki-ki-ki-ki-ki-ki-ki.*

Petri

NORTHERN GOSHAWK

Spring had found the campus of Alaska Pacific University playing host to a pair of nesting northern goshawks. Students and professors alike soon became targets of the female's fury as she fiercely guarded her territory. A screeching *ack-ack-ack* warning often came too late for the hapless intruders she dive-bombed on campus trails. Meanwhile, in her nest, three downy chicks begged raucously for food.

No one witnessed what befell the female northern goshawk that day. When the jogger found her, her left wing hung misshapen and useless. Unable any longer to care for herself or her nestlings, and with an aggressive wildness about her that would endanger any caretaker, the hawk was given an injection that mercifully took her life.

To try to save the young goshawks' lives, Kerry Seifert and two other Anchorage falconers were called in to provide them homes. Licensed by the U.S. Fish and Wildlife Service to train and hunt with falcons, Kerry would become a caretaker to one of the fuzzy white bundles with gangly feet and a polished dark beak. He nicknamed the little bird Petri.

That night, in Kerry's living room, Petri settled into his new nesting area. Snuggled safely into a cardboard box, his hunger quieted by pieces of a defrosted quail, he prepared for a nap much like a human baby would do. Feet stretched straight behind him, Petri nestled on his stomach, finding the most comfortable position. Spreading his stubby wings to each side, he gave a careful look around the room before closing his pale blue eyes.

As the weeks passed, Petri grew rapidly. The white fluff gave way to sleek brown feathers, and the blue eyes turned a piercing yellow, following with lightning speed any and all movements. Petri had graduated from his cardboard box to a roomy wire pen in Kerry's yard and was clumsily discovering nature's gift of flight. Short hops from his perch soon turned into sustained bursts of airborne joy.

Petri was now able to feed himself independently. Quail no longer had to be cut up for him; he had learned to use his powerful talons and beak in concert to dine. Not only did he eat the choicest morsels, but he consumed all parts of the prey— including feathers, feet, and bones. Leftovers are not common when a goshawk feeds.

Normally birds "imprint" permanently on the person who raises them in captivity, accepting that person as a surrogate parent. Kerry had become the most important figure in Petri's life at a crucial stage in his development. This usually renders futile any attempts to release a bird back to the wild. But Petri would prove to be an exception to the rule. By the next spring, he began showing signs of the wildness he surely inherited from his spirited mother. Sensing the fierceness in this young bird's nature, Kerry made the decision to return Petri to those of his own kind.

Falconers use the term "hacking" to describe an age-old technique for returning immature birds to the wild. After they have fledged and are ready to fly, the youngsters are released into a safe yard. A platform, called a "hack," is erected for their food, and frozen quail are offered. Eventually the birds start disappearing on hunting forays of their own, returning after a day or two to the hack. These trips gradually become longer and longer, as the birds move closer to claiming their independence.

At first, Petri remained near the only home he remembered. Yet, as summer slipped away, he began exploring the limits of the legendary flying ability possessed by all hawks. Eventually he failed to return at all to the hack in Kerry's yard. Petri had no need of the food provided there. He was hunting on his own and was wild once more.

By nature, northern goshawks are reclusive birds, not often seen outside the forests where they live and hunt. The next winter, when Kerry noticed a mature goshawk perched confidently in a tree close to the house, he stared in amazement. Resting quietly, the raptor gazed at the falconer for what seemed like a magically long moment. Then he slowly unfolded his great wings and lifted off, circling higher and higher. Perhaps a mature and healthy northern goshawk had come back for a brief visit to the spot where he first learned to be free.

NORTHERN GOSHAWK (Accipiter gentilis)
> Size: 19 inches long; 42-inch wingspan.
> Identifying characteristics: Broad rounded wings, long tail, dark hooked beak.
> Plumage: Blackish head, gray back and underwings, broad white eye stripe.
> Diet: Mostly birds, sometimes small mammals.
> Range: Alaska, Canada, continental United States as far as southern Texas.
> Habitat: Mainly woodlands and forests.
> Nesting habits: Builds a nest of sticks; prefers trees; reuses nests for years.
> Clutch size: Typically 2 to 4 eggs; incubation time of 36 to 38 days.
> Voice: Sharp, screeching *ack-ack-ack.*

Cheerful

BLACK-CAPPED CHICKADEE

Three small chickadees peered from their nest into the eyes of their rescuers. Children at play had discovered the birds on the ground; perhaps a windstorm had dislodged them from their tree. At the Bird TLC clinic, the babies were kept together as they grew larger and healthier. Two of the chickadees developed normally and fledged, growing the necessary tail and wing feathers that enabled them to fly. After a few weeks those two were released to the wild to join a flock of their own kind.

But the remaining chick couldn't manage to grow any decent feathers. Barbara Doak, a frequent volunteer at Bird TLC, kept a close eye on the tiny creature all that summer. Eventually, she moved the chick from the clinic to her own home, suspecting that it might need long-term care. This little bird came to be known as Cheerful. Whenever Barbara returned home from work, Cheerful's *chick-a-dee-dee-dee* would ring out in a welcoming song. She was indeed a happy, outgoing little bird.

Cheerful was a petite ball of fluff—small even by chickadee standards. With a jaunty dark cap and bib, sporting snowy cheeks and a pale underbelly, she measured even less than the normal four inches and tipped the scale at a mere one-third of an ounce. Her tail never materialized, for no sooner would the feathers grow in than they would break off or fall out. None of the quill-shaped wing feathers stayed, either. Perhaps an early nutritional deficiency was the culprit; it was impossible to know for certain.

In Barbara's sunroom, Cheerful took up residence in a roomy wire cage and explored every inch of it with unflagging energy. Sometimes, thinking she could fly, she tried leaping to perches; then—*plop*—she tumbled down. Cheerful always picked herself up without ceremony and ran to one side of the cage to start all over again.

Barbara hoped Cheerful might grow feathers when it was molting time the next spring, but no luck. Most birds molt yearly, a process that entails not only shedding old feathers but growing new ones as well. Her proper chickadee markings were present; all that was missing were tail and wing feathers.

Then, lo and behold, a tiny miracle occurred near the end of Cheerful's second summer: she grew her missing feathers. In a matter of days she was flying in her cage. By the time heavy frosts foretold late fall, Cheerful was ready to join a flock of her own kind.

Remarkably, chickadees are year-round residents in the North. To endure the long, bitter winters, they have much denser plumage than other songbirds of their size. In this way, they can effectively trap warm air close to their bodies, insulating themselves from the cold. Chickadees also have an ability to put on up to eight percent of their body weight in fat each day. This would be the same as a 150-pound person gaining 12 pounds in twenty-four hours. During the evening, the tiny birds utilize this fat as fuel. By dropping their body temperature at the same time, much as a ground squirrel would do, chickadees additionally conserve energy to help them survive the arctic nights.

Another Bird TLC volunteer, who lives on a wooded Anchorage hillside, provides sunflower seeds and suet year-round to a flock of wild chickadees. Such flocks usually consist of several adult pairs and unrelated juveniles. It was close to this volunteer's brimming feeder that Barbara placed Cheerful's cage and opened the wire door. Able to come and go at will, she soon joined the other birds in flitting hunts for the insects and larvae that composed most of their diet. After only a few days, Cheerful was a fully accepted member of the flock.

She has remained a faithful resident ever since. Because she is louder than the other chickadees, her voice is easy to pick out. Tamer than most, she occasionally lights close by when the feeder is filled with the prized black seeds she relishes.

The spring after her release, Cheerful was accompanied by three babies at the feeder. Mirroring her sunny disposition in their bright songs and energy, the chicks were already well on their way to mastering the acrobatic flights they would need as adults. A glance showed clearly, too, that their tiny wings and tails were already perfectly feathered for the job.

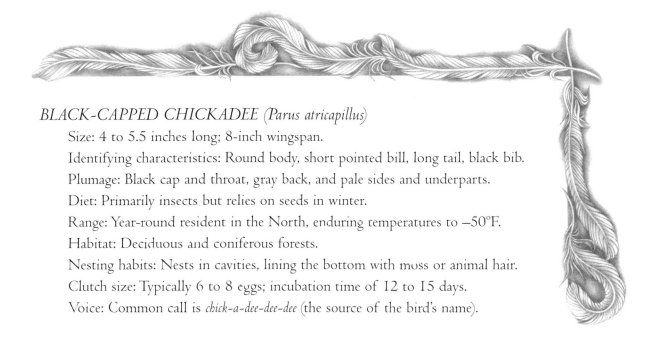

BLACK-CAPPED CHICKADEE (Parus atricapillus)
Size: 4 to 5.5 inches long; 8-inch wingspan.
Identifying characteristics: Round body, short pointed bill, long tail, black bib.
Plumage: Black cap and throat, gray back, and pale sides and underparts.
Diet: Primarily insects but relies on seeds in winter.
Range: Year-round resident in the North, enduring temperatures to −50°F.
Habitat: Deciduous and coniferous forests.
Nesting habits: Nests in cavities, lining the bottom with moss or animal hair.
Clutch size: Typically 6 to 8 eggs; incubation time of 12 to 15 days.
Voice: Common call is *chick-a-dee-dee-dee* (the source of the bird's name).

EPILOGUE

The Legacy of One Wing

On June 3, 1990, nine bald eagles rescued from the 1989 *Exxon Valdez* oil spill had recovered sufficiently to be released and were waiting uneasily in their cages on the shores of Prince William Sound near Cordova. Bird TLC volunteers carefully lifted them out one by one and attached hoods to help keep the birds calm. A healthy bald eagle is a formidable creature, and holding one still is no easy task—especially for the half-hour it takes to epoxy a tail-feather transmitter in place. Absorbing the sun's warmth along with the humans, the eagles were sweating in the afternoon heat. Salty droplets trickled down foreheads and beaks alike.

After workers lowered each bird gently to the ground, they pulled off its hood. Each in turn, the eagles felt the cool pebbles and gritty volcanic sand underfoot and soon realized that freedom was there for the taking. Hopping clumsily forward one foot at a time, they appeared to be playing a spirited game of hopscotch. A moment later, they spread their huge, graceful wings and fled from the beach, leaving sanctuary and their rescuers far below.

Nearly all of these powerful birds had received life-saving transfusions of blood from One Wing, the maimed eagle no one had expected to survive.

In the dark months after the oil spill, months filled with media images of poisoned and dying creatures, the release of nine healthy, rehabilitated bald eagles was good news. It gave tangible proof of the resilience of wildlife and the determination to survive that is inherent in all living things. It also was a tribute to the many volunteers who had invested countless hours to make the release a reality. They had given of their time expecting no thanks other than the chance to see wild birds fly free again. The years separating the spill from the present have seen those same volunteers, and many new ones, continue the healing work born of that environmental disaster.

One Wing still resides in Bird TLC's flight pens at Fort Richardson. Unbowed by the captivity that was not of his own choosing, and healthy except for his missing wing, he retains his strong spiritedness.

The Old Witch, an imposing female, has shared a pen with One Wing for many years. Larger than her mate, as female raptors usually are, she has a wildness about her that has never softened. "If you need to catch The Old Witch for any reason," says Dr. Jim Scott, "you'd better be prepared to be torn up a bit!" He chuckles as he speaks of her. The fire and defiance that glow in her are traits he admires.

Often, through the years, One Wing and The Old Witch have shared their enclosure temporarily with other recovering bald eagles, ones that will eventually be released with good wishes and high expectations for long, independent lives. Yet this special pair, who must always stay behind, have been more than just earth-bound survivors. They have truly been symbols of hope and inspiration, touching many people's lives in unforgettable ways.

Artist's Notes

I work primarily in pencil, a medium that I've favored for thirty years. The simplicity of the graphite allows for painstaking detail and photo-realistic quality. To preserve that detail in these illustrations, the color was not added directly to the originals, but instead "painted" on a transparent film overlay with pastel dust, a technique that many scientific illustrators use. I have tried to accurately draw these birds as they are, and not gloss over the injuries or less than perfect feathers, and I hope their individuality shines through. The art has really been by far the most fun and the most meaningful thing for me—it has been a joy.

Several artists have influenced my work. Garry Kaulitz, an immensely talented illustrator and printmaker, nudged me to explore new techniques. Gerald Hodge, a master of scientific illustration, amazes me. Ray Troll's art continually delights me. June Mullins, my gifted twin sister, inspires me.

List of illustrations:

Cover. One Wing. At first I had thought it might be too shocking for people to see One Wing on the cover. Though the area where the wing has been amputated is covered with fuzzy feathers and, of course, completely healed, it's nevertheless a very unusual thing to see a bird with only one wing. I went to the flight pens and used a telephoto lens to get some expressive and detailed shots of One Wing to use as material for this illustration.

Title Page. Eagle. I drew this portrait from a photograph by Danny Simmons, who took the picture in the early 1990s when this eagle was under the care of Bird TLC. I've always loved its fierce look.

Contents Page. These three baby chickadees were drawn from a photograph taken by Dr. Jim Scott.

They still had their down and fluffy feathers at this stage, and one was especially sleepy. They were brought into the bird rescue center as fledglings and later released when they were able to fly.

Page 4. Introduction. This is Little Babe, the warbler, rendered from a photo by Barbara Doak, who took the bird into her home after treatment at Bird TLC.

Page 8. See Cover.

Page 12. Corbie. I created this drawing using several photos that I had taken as resource materials. Corbie has a badly damaged wing, which is obvious in the drawing. He is an outgoing and social bird, however, and seems to enjoy posing for photographs. He didn't mind the flash bulb at all.

Page 16. Chitina. Danny Simmons supplied a photograph of Chitina for reference for this illustration. Taken in the early 1990s, it graphically displays the drooping wing that was injured.

Page 20. Grumpy. Until Grumpy's death in 1998, Barbara Doak took care of him. He was elderly and quite dignified, and posed beautifully for the camera when I visited Barbara to get some photos of him. Though this particular drawing doesn't make it obvious, one of his wings had been amputated due to a shooting many years earlier.

Page 24. Blue. This Steller's jay has a useless wing from an old injury, and the illustration shows that abnormality. The olives in the border depict Blue's favorite food. It was difficult to get a detailed photo of Blue, as he is very active and isn't concerned about staying still for the camera. I ended up making this drawing from a composite of photos that I had taken at Barbara Doak's house, where Blue resides.

Page 28. Little Babe. This drawing was made from detailed photos that Barbara Doak loaned me. Little Babe had a tiny spot of white feathers on her head, which is visible in the drawing. She died several years ago, so I had to rely solely on photographs.

Page 32. Healy. I made this drawing from several photos that I took at Alex Carter's house one cold winter afternoon. Wayne Rush was caring for Healy while Alex was away and I tagged along with my camera. Healy didn't mind at all, and posed for me uncomplainingly. He is an enormous bird and his coloration is stunning.

Page 36. Carroll. This eagle was drawn from a photo that William Amos took at Homer, Alaska, in the early 1990s. While it isn't specifically a portrait of Carroll, I hope it captures the breathless beauty of a rehabilitated bald eagle as it's released back to the wild.

Page 40. Ravenhood. I photographed Ravenhood in the mid-1990s as reference for this drawing. He poses very readily and it was a sunny day, so I was able to get a lot of the detail in his black feathers. I tried to capture his outgoing personality and curious nature.

Page 44. Valentine. I was lacking any images of Valentine, so I drew this from an image of another gyrfalcon photographed by Danny Simmons. This bird is depicted on the glove. I believe it adds a human element to the drawing, and also is an accurate representation, since many of these birds are trained to the glove so they can be used for educational purposes.

Page 48. Jewel. I used several of my own photo studies for this drawing. Jewel is cared for by Wayne and Judy Rush, and has a severely damaged wing, which renders her nonreleasable.

Page 52. Petri. I believe Petri was about two months old when I took the photo for this illustration. Kerry Seifert allowed me to photograph him at regular intervals from the time he was a white fluff ball until he was a mature-looking goshawk. Shortly after I took this photo, Petri flew over and sat on my head, a rather startling experience. Fortunately, he didn't harm me with his talons, but just sat there a minute. I was surprised at how heavy he was.

Page 56. Cheerful. Created from a photograph by Barbara Doak, this illustration depicts Cheerful when she was still very young, barely past fledgling stage and not yet able to fly.

Page 60. Epilogue. This is one of my favorites, drawn from a photo taken by Richard Bass. He photographed this eagle in Homer, Alaska, in the late 1980s. I added the salmon wreath, as bald eagles love to eat salmon and the design of the fish heads was an interesting contrast to the bird.